RASHAD HO

The FIVE
LENSES

The Five Lenses®

Table of Contents

CHAPTER 1

Anger is Inspiration.
Inspiration is Transformation.

"Invention, it must be humbly admitted, does not consist in creating out of void, but out of chaos

-Mary Wollenstonecraft Shelley

I was in Omaha, Nebraska in a hotel room with my business partner Donte Tanner after dinner and a nightcap at a hookah lounge. We'd had a few drinks already and were accessing the additional "courage" that comes from those drinks to address our concerns about our team members serving one of our Department of Defense (DoD) clients.

"I just feel like we have the wrong people," he exclaimed as we talked through the moment. I was incredibly sensitive about the people I'd hired. Thus, I interpreted his statement as a personal attack, and was on the defensive as I calculated my response.

Incredulous, I asked him what he meant by "wrong people". He explained that we had hired people with skills I was expecting to help *develop* in order to fit the roles, but not people who had the skills <u>and</u> already understood all the work they were doing.

"I've worked with many of the best consulting firms in the country," I replied "and few of them have the 'right people' in the 'right roles' if we're going by that." I'm sure I replied by telling him that *he* was the problem and that he needed to adjust *his* management style and expectations.

He responded by asking me a simple question that stopped me in my tracks and shifted my anger to indignation. "Since you like helping people so much, and we both agree that you do it, often to your detriment, have **you** "helped" them understand all they need in order to be successful? Since I have to manage them, and you've left me with that responsibility without wanting me to raise the standard, have you even helped them enough to perform to the *basic* standard? Do they know what they need to know...from YOU?"

I didn't answer it directly, and likely misdirected the conversation away from his specific question, because I knew the answer. The answer was...*I don't know.* When both of us were tired (it was 3am and we had an early morning flight back to Washington, DC), we finally stopped arguing and went to sleep. When we woke up, we'd squashed the argument, but his question stuck with me.

When I first hired many of our team members, the majority of them were former colleagues or were referrals (friends) of my former colleagues. Because I'd worked with many of the team members before, I'd *assumed* they'd been exposed to how program management offices were staffed and were supposed to work. I likewise assumed they recognized what was important about their current work as I had lightly touched on those items of critical importance during their interviews. When I onboarded each of them, I thought I'd done an adequate job of describing the customer(s) they'd support; the numerous customer issues that needed resolving; and the roles/titles they would fill to address those customer issues. I also assumed that my previous actions had provided enough context for both how the organization was set up, and the rules of engagement for how they were to operate within it. I couldn't answer Donte's question in that moment, however, because I realized in that moment that I'd only assumed my previous actions indeed were enough, but had never really confirmed with anyone whether they truly understood those things.

The next morning I'd planned to sleep on the plane ride, but couldn't. I was brooding at my inability to answer Donte's question. I was upset with myself, but was also still (irrationally) upset with him for even asking it. The only thing I knew to do at the moment was to build a simple slide deck that would at least provide the answer to the question he asked me at a high level, while serving as an easy reference for my team. When I put it together, I honestly believed that what I'd written was already something everyone on the team had understood, and (deep down) I hoped they would be annoyed to have to be re-briefed. In fact, I was a bit annoyed putting it together.

As I began to draft the layout and content, I was intending to patronize the group with the level of detail I was adding to each section. In hindsight, I hate to admit that I intended for them to sense my sarcasm and feel bad for needing me to tell them the answers. I was writing, assuming they would respond by letting me know they already knew these things. I also thought the document would give me an opportunity to equitably injure Donte's ego in response to how much he'd succeeded in injuring mine hours before. When I was finished with the presentation, just before we landed, I showed my work to him, proud of myself for what I thought would be making an obvious point. To my surprise, he offered his approval, provided a few points of feedback, and encouraged me to present it to the team later that day. That afternoon, I presented my team with **The Five Swimlanes** in a presentation titled "Portfolio Management Framework".

Portfolio Management Framework

People & Culture	Strategy	Operations & Oversight	Governance	Innovation & Technology
Team Lead:	Team Lead:	Team Lead:	Team Lead:	Team Lead:
RH	EB	DT	VW	AS

Figure 1.1 - The Five Swimlanes Portfolio Management Framework (slide 1 - circa June 2015)

I presented Figure 1 above and walked through (in as condescending a tone as I could muster) the Five Swimlanes. All of the activities and functions we were expected to execute in our daily work for our customer were organized into one of those swimlanes. I went through each of those functions in detail and described why I felt those functions belonged in that swimlane, and how the activities in those lanes contributed to and were interdependent with the activities in the other lanes. On the second slide of that presentation (Figure 1.2) I described how our team structure could be organized into each of those lanes, and assigned team leads for each lane. During the presentation I answered questions team members had about where and how they could add value within those swim lanes, and clarified some of the terms for which they needed clarification. At the end of the presentation and meeting, the response was bittersweet. The team members expressed their appreciation for the clarity and structure. They further expressed that they each felt more comfortable as the presentation and conversation outlined work they thought was tangible and measurable, as well as clarified the people to whom they could report and get validation for successful completion of that work.

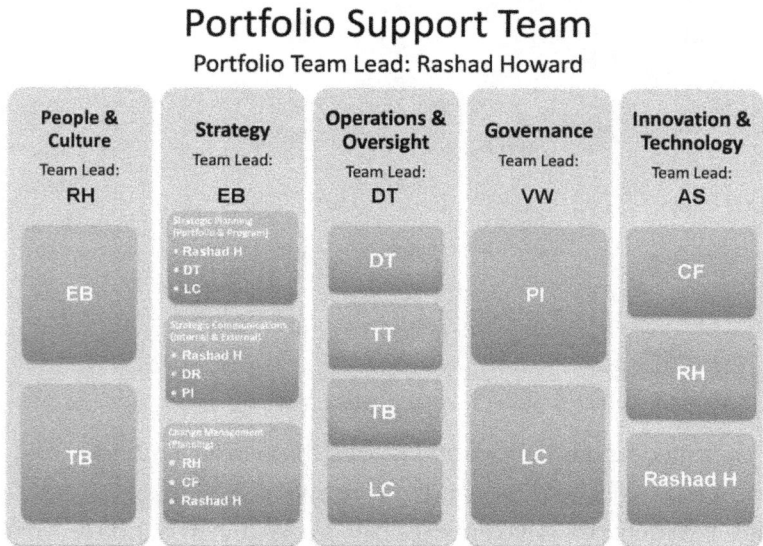

Portfolio Support Team
Portfolio Team Lead: Rashad Howard

People & Culture	Strategy	Operations & Oversight	Governance	Innovation & Technology
Team Lead: RH	Team Lead: EB	Team Lead: DT	Team Lead: VW	Team Lead: AS
EB	Strategic Planning (Portfolio & Program) • Rashad H • DT • LC	DT	PI	CF
	Strategic Communications (Internal & External) • Rashad H • DR • PI	TT		RH
TB	Change Management (Planning) • RH • CF • Rashad H	TB	LC	Rashad H
		LC		

Figure 1.2 - The Five Swimlanes team member assignments (Slide 2 - Circa June 2015)

None of them seemed to feel as if I had been patronizing. Most of them felt as though I'd finally given them *useful* guidance that would help them be successful. Some of them expressed that they were impressed that I'd finally shown them that I, in fact, had a plan (they'd previously questioned that) and (even worse) had clearly shown them that I knew what I was doing. All of them made it clear: Donte was right.

It was one of the best (and worst) days of my career as a consulting "leader".

CHAPTER **2**

Simplicity is Power

"Simplicity is the ultimate sophistication."

- Leonardo da Vinci

What is undeniably important about that day, however, is that our whole team was able to move forward with clarity, each person understanding their roles within the portfolio staff as well as their orientation to others on the team. Our conversations with our customer and the program managers who reported to him were much simpler as well. We found that the Five Swimlanes became a tool that allowed for safer communication, and a grounding of sorts when faced with frustrating, complex, and/or ambiguous program issues.

There was also an elegance that accompanied its simplicity. There were only five lanes (later renamed "lenses") to remember. When explaining them in meetings where we didn't have the benefit of projecting slides onto a screen, we could simply explain them using the fingers on one hand. In fact, for fun, we could even communicate the value of each lens using anecdotes for each finger.

The thumb, for instance, was the "most important" representing the strength, grip, and functionality of the whole hand, essentially going as far as saying it gave value to it as the hand couldn't really function without it. Thus, the thumb represented "People & Culture".

The index finger, the one that "points" us forward to our destination...or, points in the sky (up the organizational hierarchy) when one asks to be "excused" (or given an excuse) represents "Strategy".

The middle finger represented operations. If the day-to-day, operational functions of your organization were out of place or inept, your organization would literally be (excuse the crudeness)..."F'd".

One of the biggest decisions in our lives is the decision to marry, and so many other life outcomes center around that **decision**, thus the "ring" finger represents "Governance".

Finally, the least important, yet still needed function was the technology or tools we use to work, thus it's the pinky. Again, it serves as a simple heuristic that can easily be remembered in its elegance, and easily communicated and extended upon.

Following a suggestion from one of my senior consultants at the time (Mark Jones), I later changed the name from the Five Swimlanes, to the Five Lenses®. Mark had always felt uncomfortable calling them lanes because he felt that a "lane" connoted something one should "stay within" and that the tool (especially if you follow our "hand" example above) should better communicate interdependence. He felt that people in organizations already had issues *focusing* too much in their own silos and it was important that we didn't further that behavior. He suggested replacing swimlanes with lenses, as he saw each *lens* as a tool for us to gain a particular *perspective* within an organization. He also rightly tapped into the deep metaphor around sight and vision as more appropriate, as the Five Lenses could be used as an analytical tool to gain "insights" into organizations.

The name change was one of many iterations and adjustments we made to the Five Lenses in implementation. While the tool was originally applied as a simple way to organize work functions and human resources to staff a Portfolio Management Office, its simplicity allowed us to extend it into a transformative framework for understanding organizational design; assessing organizational and program performance; conducting root cause analyses; and inspiring strategic thinking and behaviors that promote seamless alignment with strategic organizational objectives. It also has become incredibly useful in unearthing organizational pain points and concerns previously unnamed or unrecognized, but that critically impact overall organizational success.

As my team members and I became more entrenched in commercial client advisory and PMO support for public sector clients, we continued to evolve the concept, even experimenting at times with additional factors. This heuristic could easily have expanded to seven, eight, or nine lenses, but our iterations and retrospectives led us back to the same five areas that persist in the Five Lenses Framework to this day:

- People & Culture
- Strategy
- Operations
- Governance
- Technology

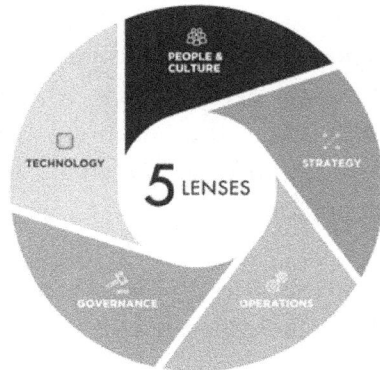

The Five Definitions

The Five Lenses is ultimately a simple heuristic...a kind of "precise enough" tool. The definitions for each of the lenses loosely describe how we intend the lenses to be applied, but are not entirely prescriptive. You may extend upon, or better yet, simplify these definitions to drive their use as powerful communication tools within your own organizations or with your own clients. My team has iterated on these definitions multiple times in efforts to create a shared lexicon of understanding between our clients and themselves. I personally keep the definitions rather broad so that the appropriate fidelity and rigidity can be applied in the appropriate circumstances. The beauty of a heuristic like this is that it is an adaptive framework that can be cross-applied to many situations. Use these definitions to get you started:

People & Culture - Humans that make up the organization and the cultural effects of those humans' execution of the other four lenses

Organizations are simply collections of people doing work. This lens describes the people who make up the organization; the ways in which they interact; the confidence with which they do their work; and structures in place to help them continue to be valuable and grow within the organization.

Strategy - The philosophy, thinking, and decisions about why the organization exists; what it does; and who it will serve in order to succeed. These "strategic" decisions drive every other organizational activity: planning; goals/objectives-setting activities, processes and practices alignment; and marketing & communications activities.

This lens describes the strategic orientation, position, and foci of an organization to include being explicit about the organization's value proposition. Good strategy requires us to understand and explicitly define what "success" means to the organization. The strategy lens is also the lens within which we make decisions that drive how we operate; how we will be organized to operate effectively; and how we will market and communicate internally to our team members, as well as externally to our key partners, stakeholders, and customers.

Any qualitative analysis in the strategy lens includes determining if the organization has a clear description for why it exists; whether decisions have been made for exactly what is the organization's value proposition; to whom the organization provides this clearly-stated and understood value (as well as to whom it will NOT provide this value); whether there are agreed-upon and documented near and longer-term plans (goals and objectives) for delivering that value; whether there are metrics to measure the success of those near and long-term plans, and to what extent those plans have been communicated within and outside of the organization.

Operations - The processes, practices, and procedures people follow to produce what the organization produces, even if the "product" is a service. Simply put, this lens describes how work is done within the organization.

The operations lens includes the day-to-day processes, procedures, practices, and infrastructure that keep an organization operating in support of its strategy. Another way to describe operations is that it describes the things the "real workers" are *doing* to meet the named objectives of the organization...the daily business activities outside of planning/thinking (strategy) and decision-making (governance). For simplicity, we include all relevant day-to-day activities that support the organization's ability to provide value to customers (including financial operations) within this lens.

Governance - The decision-making infrastructure of an organization. This includes any councils, working groups, boards, or persons-in-authority, as well as the documents, memos, and policies that outline who and how decisions are/will be made.

At its core, this is the hierarchical set-up people within the organization must navigate for major decisions within the other lenses. Major strategic objectives that are planned ultimately must be considered and approved by the decision-making infrastructure, be it a single person, a combination of executives or managers, and/or a board (or set of boards or working groups) consensus vote. Simply put, the governance lens addresses how decisions are made and through which organizational bodies information must flow before a decision is made, communicated, and complied with.

Technology - The tools used by the people within the organization to engage in daily operations and/or produce the organization's product or service. Simply put, these are the tools the organization must use to create value.

This is generally meant to describe the tangible tools, hardware, and/or software with which people in the organization interact and that supports those peoples' abilities to accomplish operational, strategic, or governance duties/tasks/responsibilities, etc.

CHAPTER **3**

The Case for the Five Lenses®

"If it's broke, fix it!"

- Cheryl Davis (my mother)

As I was gaining early experience in providing support to clients as a consultant, I found myself pursuing and obtaining advanced certifications in project management, and eventually worked as a project manager on multiple engagements. My career progression eventually led to me being placed in roles where I was asked to create staffing plans for project (or program) management offices (PMOs) for specific engagements. Initial staffing attempts followed traditional project management staff guidelines, and most clients were satisfied with the traditional staffing mix, particularly since the staffing plans matched what they'd become familiar with themselves.

Along the way, however, I found my customers growing more frustrated with their programs' performance despite their PMO teams being properly staffed with certified and seasoned program managers (and other seasoned team members) adhering to traditional project management guidelines. Those traditional teams "managed" the *cost, schedule, and scope* (also known as the "triple constraint") of projects in accordance with everything they'd learned through experiences and project management certification programs, yet were still experiencing significant failures. In fact the **failure rates for projects** (depending on the source of the research and statistics) in 2015 were generally cited to be **above 70%,** all failing to be on time, on budget, or to meet client satisfaction goals (Chaos 2015), with some reports citing that 44% of projects failed to even align with the strategic goals and intent of the project (PMI 2014). Simply put, **the classical project management approach** (despite its pervasiveness in use, and the multitude of certification and continuing education programs built around it) **failed in practice**, and it was particularly underperforming in managing government technology programs.

The Vulnerability of the Triple Constraint

One of the unique issues we experience in serving customers in the public sector is to expertly evaluate **program** or **portfolio performance**. The tools and processes we used to provide performance management were traditionally meant to support **projects**, and mainly projects within non-government organizations. The problem, however, is that projects are expected to be finite, having a definite beginning and end, and are to have explicit, predetermined goals with easy-to-define metrics that align with predefined outcomes. These outcomes are often things like:

- Some percentage increase/decrease in revenue/profit
- Some X number increase/decrease of widgets built to meet some specified productivity goal
- Some X amount of positive versus negative responses on a survey from some stakeholder/customer organization directly impacted by that project/initiative

Programs, however, are a *series* of related and often *ongoing* projects or initiatives meant to deliver defined value to singular or multiple customers and stakeholders. Programs can provide one or many value propositions to those customers and stakeholders, and what is considered value (as well as who are considered customers or stakeholders) can shift over time. These potential shifts tell us the resources, processes, practices, people, technologies, decisions, messages, skill sets, and plans (amongst other things) are also shifting within the organization and must all be understood in real-time as factors that drive the shifts in what is considered value and to whom. These are some of the dynamic, core factors named and tracked within the Five Lenses while the elements of the triple constraint simply manifest as static symptoms of these underlying, dynamic factors.

Why the Triple Constraint Breaks Down

We found the vulnerabilities of the triple constraint particularly insufficient in managing technology programs and portfolios within the Department of Defense. The reasons for this insufficiency are numerous, but it is particularly true given the nature of how federal programs are budgeted for, funded, and supported over time.

Federal government program managers work in a system where their executive leadership expects them to budget by submitting budget requests that cover multiple fiscal years. When the requests are submitted, program managers have to estimate potential costs for future years' requirements. This means these program managers and their organizational leaders are beholden to budget requests that may not account for potential changes in organizational needs, market changes, or potential crises.

To add insult to injury, federal government program managers are expected to expend all of the funds that were allocated for their program for a given fiscal year within that same fiscal year. When these funds are not expended in their entirety, for any reason, those funds have to be "returned" for reallocation to other organizational priorities, or eventually to the US Treasury rather than carried over for the PM to use in the next fiscal year.

When this happens, program managers are often "punished" by having their future budgets cut in accordance with the same percentage of the unexpended funds they returned to their agencies. This means that even if the program manager experienced cost savings due to efficient management and good stewardship, their future budget could be cut, potentially diminishing their ability to steward their program with adequate resources in the next fiscal year.

Overall this means program managers in the public sector are incentivized only to expend their entire budgets to avoid future cuts. Their leaders then determine the standard for "good" cost performance as simply a measure of whether the PM is on track to expend all of their budgeted funds in a fiscal year versus determining whether the government is receiving the optimal value for the expended funds.

Thus, the cost component of the triple constraint in these scenarios neither provides any indication of the extent to which the program is delivering its intended value for its costs, nor does it measure how well the program manager is stewarding those resources to provide that value. It also doesn't tell us *why* the funds expended are (or are not) sufficient for the program to provide its intended value. This lack of insight from this measure creates a net lose-lose scenario for the program manager; their team members who deliver value within the program; the customers at the receiving end of program's service (or lack thereof); the portfolio or agency senior leaders responsible for program oversight; and for those (who often have to answer to Congress) who are responsible for prioritizing budget allocations to agencies.

Another issue is how the schedule is evaluated. When senior executives decry timelines for specific initiatives within the programs, government program managers often have to game the reporting process by simply re-baselining the schedule, thereby erasing any indications of schedule "overruns". The same is often said with scope given that as a schedule is re-baselined, scope items are generally dropped or added in accordance with whatever can be agreed upon as acceptable within new schedule timeframes.

The triple constraint alone left program managers and portfolio managers equally confused when mission objectives and/or stakeholder needs were left unmet. Our team members regularly attended (and still do today) meetings where Program Managers would be admonished for poor program "performance" even though their presentation briefing slides would report that they were "green" (performing as planned) in the areas of cost, schedule, and scope. They had effectively expended their entire budget, which, of course, is a necessary action to secure future funds for the entire portfolio. They had also effectively re-baselined their schedules to show that all "deliverables" would be accomplished "on schedule" (again, performing as planned). Lastly, they had re-aligned work packets such that all items being worked and activities performed were "in scope" (as planned). Though these "as planned" reports allowed for reporting good news and "green" statuses on a stoplight chart[1], the programs were regularly seen as failing and/or not meeting mission requirements by sponsors and stakeholders either in function(s), value proposition(s), and measurements of return on investment (ROI).

Moving Through Stoplights

We worked closely with a DoD client who was a portfolio manager who wanted to address the issue of his program managers' consistent "green" stoplight reports, despite his constantly receiving angry messages from his bosses and the "customers" whose missions were negatively impacted by his programs' poor performances. When he would question his program managers (PMs) about the issues he was being asked to address, their responses would exacerbate his frustration. They would often point to issues that were, as far as they were concerned, outside their locus of control:

---

1   In management consulting, stoplight **charts** are used to indicate status of risks, or trends in overall project performance. The color displays (typically) red, yellow, and green usually represent likelihood or level of risk and/or serve as negative/neutral/positive trend indicators of overall project performance. Many organizations have extended their use as a "dashboard" that alerts decision makers about what - and to what degree - an issue should be addressed. "Green" status usually means things are going or trending well; yellow describes that something needs further attention; and red indicates that something needs to be urgently fixed or is beyond mitigation. Stoplight charts as management tools often lead to organizational "gaming" where those who are reporting status always want to figure out what is necessary to make their status items consistently "green" to avoid negative consequences.

The customers are always shifting requirements, but not being realistic about the accompanying shift in resources and time necessary to address their requirements

The customers simply don't know what they want, and since they don't know what they want they're blaming us for their own inability to meet their mission

I don't understand what the problem is, or why anyone is complaining. We've expended our budget, and we've delivered a set of capabilities within scope and on schedule. I'm not responsible for making the customers do a good job at their own work.

No, I don't know when my vendor contracts expire. Isn't the contracting office supposed to know that and tell me what to do?

I don't know what budget is required. I simply look at the list of requirements from the functional customers and ask my vendors for a cost proposal to meet those requirements. If I don't get the money for that, it's not my fault.

It's not my fault, we did everything we could to accommodate the customer's needs, plus my slides show that my program is "Green".

I don't know when our vendor contracts expire, so I don't know if our current support levels are truly at risk

Our support levels are at risk and our contracts expire TOMORROW.

*No, I don't have a strategic plan for this. Is that my job, or are the functionals (customers) supposed to tell me what **their** strategy is?*

He repeatedly asked for his program managers to "think strategically" about their programs, but was met with responses he felt lacked meaningful reflection of how their work contributed to the organization's mission. Other responses, he felt, demonstrated the program managers' lack of understanding about how their program was expected to meet their customers' needs. Still other responses, he felt, indicated his program managers' unwillingness to think deeply about how to resolve issues in program performance, and were an even deeper indication of their overall laziness as PMs.

He consolidated all these responses and his frustration into his feeling that, overall, some PMs simply lacked either the capacity (skill) or commitment (will) to think strategically about their work. Because the triple constraint was his organizations' only criteria for performance management (and was the basis upon which organizational stoplight charts were built), he had no real way to incentivize the activities and behaviors he expected to see from his program managers that would constitute "strategic thinking".

As a remedy, he asked our team to conduct some leadership training with his program managers for a few days at an off-site training session. His main objective for us was that, after teaching his PMs what it meant to be "strategic", we would facilitate strategic planning sessions where PMs could, at the very least, leave the offsite with clarity about their programs' strategic position within the portfolio. While the training provided temporary spikes in organizational morale, there was little evidence there were any sustainable organizational shifts in confidence and performance.

CHAPTER 4

Incentivizing Strategic Thinking

"Show me the incentive and I will show you the outcome."

- Charlie Munger

Despite the many lectures and training we and our customer gave proselytizing that program managers should think strategically about their programs, PMs would return to their organizations unsure of exactly *how* to execute their work "strategically". Moreover, even for those PMs who seemed to "get it," our customer had no way to measure their strategic thinking performance or progress. PMs soon saw themselves and their organizations struggling with the same customer service and mission demand issues, and for a few of the PMs, their relationships with our client (their portfolio manager and supervisor) became more contentious.

We soon realized that what was needed was a management control that incentivized the strategic thinking **behaviors** for which PMs would be **rewarded**. The portfolio manager needed a reporting system or framework that shifted each PM's focus away from color combinations on stoplight charts to more substantive, meaningful, and measurable activities that could be openly edified and rewarded as evidence of their "strategically thinking about their programs". We needed to address the issue of using overly simplistic stoplight performance charts, where PMs feel they're being measured (*judged*) by whether their charts are "green," versus being **rewarded** for the appropriate management behaviors.

A similar example of this phenomenon can be understood from the use of stoplight charts in classrooms as a way to manage and organize student behavior. The drawback being that students shift their focus to being "green" and not on developing problem solving skills to work out underlying issues with their peers or their teachers (Ginsburg).[2] In fact, traffic light behavior charts in schools are ineffective and can be harmful to students. These charts can create shame, anxiety, and a focus on external rewards rather than intrinsic motivation (Dewar)[3] (O'Brien)[4] (Causton and MacLeod)[5]

---

2   https://blogs.edweek.org/teachers/coach_gs_teaching_tips/2015/12/three_problems_with_traffic_light_behavior_charts.html
3   Dewar, Gwen. "What's wrong with classroom behavior charts: Why shaming backfires." *Parenting Science*, 2019, https://parentingscience.com/whats-wrong-with-classroom-behavior-charts/.
4   O'Brien, Jarlath. "Behaviour: why the 'traffic light' system doesn't work." *Tes*, 30 July 2021, https://www.tes.com/magazine/teaching-learning/general/behaviour-why-traffic-light-system-doesnt-work. Accessed 3 May 2023.
5   O'Brien, Jarlath. "Behaviour: why the 'traffic light' system doesn't work." *Tes*, 30 July 2021, https://www.tes.com/magazine/teaching-learning/general/behaviour-why-traffic-light-system-doesnt-work. Accessed 3 May 2023.

The "strategic thinking" our client wanted from his PMs, was the same as problem solving skills educators were hoping to incentivize students to develop. To be "strategic" as a manager was redefined as **thinking and learning through issues with** the habit of **proactive problem solving** (and problem prevention) to create value versus the habit of waiting for daily issues to arise to "put out fires" as a daily work process.

Stakeholder Satisfaction as Carrot and Stick

In some of the organizations we were servicing, we realized we were regularly seeing portfolio and program managers having to navigate responding to a new and different management control: Budget requests were approved *only* to the extent programs could prove their "customers" were satisfied. This meant that performance was being measured subjectively as a function of stakeholder satisfaction. This "measurement" and control introduced many more issues (and costs) as program managers now had to consider criteria for satisfaction that were sometimes well outside of what their program was created to address. Measuring customer satisfaction itself was, at best, a broadly subjective activity, where stakeholders mostly would respond based on how many of their personal requests were met along the way, and/or how much influence they were able to wield in having their individual groups' requirements prioritized. Said differently, a nebulous "satisfaction" rating became a tool highly influential stakeholders would use to "get their way" and curry favor with their own user community (functional/business owner/customer/stakeholders), even though prioritizing and satisfying their individual requirements might have offered little or no ROI (or worst, was detrimental) to the overall program or initiative.

The Five Lenses served as a more organized way to categorize the activities necessary to ultimately meet "mission" objectives, and to even better evaluate and prioritize customer "requirements" as they were being submitted. In a future volume, I will go into greater detail on how this may be specifically achieved using the later-developed SAGE methodology, but, at a high level, the "mission" objectives and the requirements are both individually analyzed using the Five Lenses.

For every identified mission objective (either known or identified through a discovery process) we can determine the degree to which the objective aligns with or addresses an identified organizational strategic objective. We could determine at that moment if the organization has adequately articulated - through consistent communications and memos, written and discussed policies, corporate briefings, etc. - its major strategic objectives and initiatives, along with what problems the objectives and their initiatives are meant to address. We may use these criteria and others to analyze objectives within the Strategy lens.

We can then take those same objectives and determine whether the team members in the organization understand the objectives, and more importantly, understand their individual and collective roles and responsibilities in executing those objectives. Are the team members adequately trained and possess the skill sets to address the objectives? Are plans being developed to help them develop and grow their skills to become more efficient in meeting mission objectives. Have we culturally (through our systems of measurement, controls, policies, rewards, and corrections) cultivated the atmosphere within which those team members are empowered to meet mission objectives. Are all team members able to hold each other accountable? These are some of the standards (and there are many others) used to analyze the objectives within the People & Culture lens.

Assuming we understand and address competency and role clarity challenges, do the team members have business processes, practices, and the financial structures that optimally support and advance the mission? Does the organization's budgetary and investment models enhance or hinder the ability to meet mission objectives? Are the current business processes streamlined or complex and cumbersome to implement? Have they been documented and periodically revisited as the organizational climate shifts, and/or as the organization's needs (or mission) shifts? *Are those processes and practices **driving requirements**,* or are a significant percentage of the requirements merely reactions to more immediate annoyances or "fires" that don't meaningfully serve, **enhance, or advance the mission** in any real way? These are some of the ways we would analyze objectives using the Operations lens.

Have all of the "mission's" stakeholders had adequate input, or are they regularly engaged in driving the organization's mission objectives? Are the right mix of stakeholders and sponsors (and "customers') empowered and engaged in the various councils, working groups, and decision groups to drive and approve requirements? Is there a clear decision maker in the organization responsible for executing their duties to decide when and how to meet milestones, and holding themselves accountable for outcomes? Are the rules that govern what decisions can be made at what levels of the organization clear, and is everyone who participates in the decision infrastructure clear on their role? Again, these criteria broadly help us analyze objectives using the Governance lens.

Finally, do the technologies currently in use adequately support the team members' abilities to effectively and efficiently do their jobs? Do the technologies themselves support an optimized business environment, or do the technologies create or support additional bureaucratic roadblocks? Are the technologies in play being upgraded to address the organization's challenges, or simply being upgraded on the vendor's schedule with no regard to the organization's specific objectives? Are the technologies simple to implement with current team members and, likewise, simple and intuitive enough for new team members to begin using it to effectively exercise their responsibilities in meeting the mission? These and many more questions help to analyze mission objectives through the Technology lens.

This quick five lens analysis on the front-end of the objectives themselves allow for more clear, measurable criteria for "customer satisfaction". In the example above, the degree to which program outcomes successfully meet mission objectives is heavily weighted amongst the criteria for customer satisfaction. This allows for a PM to understand specifically what challenges (within which lens) must be addressed to move the needle of 'satisfaction' versus focusing on validating reactionary (and sometimes arbitrary) requirements that serve merely as band-aids for deeper organizational wounds.

The practice of using the Five Lenses as an analysis tool eventually led my team to creating scorecards for program evaluation and performance management. Because there are nuanced differences between projects, programs, and portfolios[6] - projects having a definite beginning and end; programs being a series of ongoing activities and projects accomplishing an overall goal; and a portfolio a conglomerate of projects and programs under the same oversight and management - the

---

6   A **project** is an endeavor undertaken by an organization that has a definite end. It has a specific goal and specific resources, budget, and people assigned to help it meet that goal. A **program** is a group of related projects that are collectively managed to accomplish a mission. A **portfolio** is a collection of programs that may or may not be related to one another, yet must be managed strategically to meet overall organizational mission demands. The Five Lenses is a more robust tool for understanding and addressing the various elements that affect overall program performance beyond the triple constraint.

tools needed to measure their performance required evolution and adaptation. I was thus able to use the Five Lenses to lay the foundation for a better way to both quantitatively and qualitatively measure overall program (and thus portfolio) performance.

It also allowed us to shift the focus of managers from "how well did I do *my* part" (a type of character, competence, and value judgment of *how good they are as a PM*) to "how well are all the parts working together and where do we need to make adjustments to continue to meet mission objectives?" This shift likewise helps us shift the pressure of program performance outcomes *away from* the PM personally, allowing them to capably address specific issues that drive outcomes, versus beat themselves up when their reactions to program "fires" don't measurably improve overall program outcomes over time. It likewise, and most importantly, creates lanes of communication between the PM and their leaders for where leaders need to specifically support their PMs beyond broadly serving in an oversight role that merely judges success or failure at a perceived point in time.

CHAPTER **5**

Practice is Perfect

"The thing that hath been, it is that which shall be; and that which is done is that which shall be done: and there is no new thing under the sun."

- King Solomon, Ecclesiastes 1:19
King James Version (KJV)

There are many applications for the Five Lenses and future articles, case studies, white papers, and pamphlets will continue to provide insight into where and how they've been used to create organizational successes; build innovative software products; create artificial intelligence (AI) technologies; empower doctoral research studies; provide a planning and oversight structure for a church network; facilitate strategy making efforts in large corporations; structure business development conversations; evaluate the performance of foundation initiatives; build business cases for fundraising; categorize organizational cyber challenges; and many more. As with any tool, however, its use will both expand and evolve over time, giving us better insights into where and how it can be used.

The value in business support tools and frameworks is discovered and derived in its consistent application, and the power of the Five Lenses requires application, experimentation, adjustment, additional study, and retrospection. As of the date of this volume, I've been applying them in my consulting practices and entrepreneurial endeavors for close to 15 years. While the tool isn't a panacea for everything, it has served my clients, colleagues, and many people who I've never met incredibly well in understanding how to design and manage organizations and initiatives for which they are responsible.

I invite you to try it in your own organization or environment, and for those of you who are researchers and/or consultants, use it in your practice to offer your clients and stakeholders a more expansive option for addressing their organizational challenges. Also feel free to share your experiences with me and my team so that we can collectively add to our mutual body of knowledge and, together, improve all of our practices to better serve clients and/or meet our own organization's needs.

Acknowledgements

This content in this section is likely to be longer than some of the content in this book's chapters. I have many people to thank and a few of them for many things I likely won't be able to cover. What follows is my best attempt to acknowledge those who are specifically responsible for this work.

I'd like to first thank Donte Tanner for being a muse by any means necessary. Donte, you've always been a committed friend, a trailblazer for my ambition, and the lighthouse for me as I try to find my own way on the high seas of business. This literally would not exist without your commitment to "raise the standard" always and to always be willing to do the dirty work...and to driving the uncomfortable growth in everyone who is blessed to be in close association with you. In everything you do, continue to be a **sunray in this environment of darkness and to serve as a catalyst for change in the community.**

I'd like to thank Adarryl Roberts for believing in the power of the Five Lenses, serving as its first client advocate and for his commitment to building ecosystems where innovation and good ideas can always flourish. Without your support and commitment to holding me and my team accountable to deliver, I would never have advanced any of this, nor attempted to recruit other talented people into the circle to thoughtfully implement and evolve the framework. I also deeply appreciate the steadfast support and friendship along the way through the many twists and turns in my own practice as a consultant, entrepreneur, and human being.

I'd like to thank Vedette Gavin for your patience, kindness, friendship, trusted advisory, continuous advocacy, and willingness to resurrect things within me I once thought had little meaning or value. I also appreciate the time you've spent educating me through your lifestyle and professional endeavors on what it truly means to be 'human-centered' in my work. I could write another volume on your impact on me as a consultant, entrepreneur, executive, investor, and, most importantly, human. Everything you've taught me about anthropology and research gave me the tools to observe, analyze, and synthesize one of my recent and most important insights: you, my friend, are the North Star. Your light provides direction to all who follow for how life and work should harmonize. It's indistinguishable whether it's your life or your work that will change the world, however it is very clear that **you and your very existence as yourself** is changing the world and will continue to do so.

I'd like to thank my creative partner and brother DeWayne Jones for more than I can manage to cover in this paragraph. DeWayne, you are the greatest and most present example I have for what it looks like when one decides to engage their own genius then choose to bless those around them by teaching them to engage theirs. You have many superpowers and amongst them is your power of mining, cultivating, polishing, and amplifying everyone's genius. You bring out the best in anyone who gets close to you. Your life is the quintessential display of what it means to live in, give, and spread **love...**and to produce more love as a result. I now see myself as valuable because you encouraged me to look at myself through your lenses. As I keep looking through your lenses I start to see how you see the world and the people in it. I know the Creator cares about me every time I consider that one of the greatest blessings the Creator could have given me was your friendship.

I'd like to thank my business partner, friend, and brother Terry Rice for more than I can write here. Most important to this volume and our continued work together, however, is for teaching and inspiring me to Redefine Possible. Terry, you are the paragon for disruption and an exemplar for what it means to experience life with someone with an innovator's DNA. The world will be blessed as we experience the product(s) of your life as a few of the many mere expressions of your noble intent and commitment to leave a legacy that serves as the blueprint for those of us who want to expand beyond "building for a purpose" and into the realm of doing and being "purpose built".

I'd like to thank Alfatah "Dr. Al" Moore for brotherhood, friendship, mentorship, and partnership. At every low and high moment, you're there to propel and uplift me and everything around me. **This book exists in large part because of you**. You've served as a mentor to me in entrepreneurship, leadership, system-building, and penultimately, **genius**. All that I can accomplish today I can trace back to a moment in time when you taught me about the value of "practice" in all of life's endeavors. I love and appreciate you and consider it the honor of a lifetime to have your friendship and support; to work as a partner in thought production with you; and to live out the balance of our lives as family.

I'd like to thank Sarah "June" Benjamin who was my first writing partner and person responsible for outlining the text; validating many of my claims with research studies; and for sitting in front of me for hours encouraging me to keep writing. I likewise appreciate the many times you challenged me to think deeper about the work and for expressing the idea that the concepts themselves had universal application.

I want to thank Sade Harley for, literally, forcing me to finish this book (and everything else you force me to finish). I might have sat on this as yet another unfinished and underdeveloped idea in my hard drives if you didn't do the work of finding the resources for publishing and creating the schedules to get this across the finish line. I also greatly appreciate you for spending so much time in the gym gaining the strength to share the tremendous weight of responsibility of managing all that we are building together. You've also cured my insomnia as I no longer go to sleep stressing things I used to have to deal with on my own. Thank you for bringing peace.

I'd like to thank Brandon Wyatt for "playing defense" so well that I got extra possessions enough to score. I also thank you for your brotherhood and friendship. You have an older brother's spirit and your fearless and bold leadership inspires me to follow you even when your intention is to push from behind. Thank you for helping me to understand what is valuable and teaching me the nuances of protecting that value using official legal tools and agreements. You literally saved my business(es) multiple times through your legal and official counsel. Ultimately, however, you've saved each business by teaching me how to value and preserve all of the relationships in my life that make up those businesses, documenting the conclusions of crucial conversations in legal agreements that allow all of us to work from a foundation of trust.

I want to thank Todd Hughes for literally being a consistent life-saver and the embodiment of what it means to have someone "support" you. Todd, your attitude and approach to life, as well as your commitment to always coming through to help me start, organize, and build every business structure I can throw your way is a blessing I know I was gifted from above. I appreciate you in ways I can't always articulate, but can simply say that if there's anyone I know I can call, at any time, for anything, and count on their willingness to come in and bring their heart and talents to deliver in the greatest way possible, it's you. You ARE the Linchpin. In fact, you're no longer Todd "Money" but Todd "Linchpin". Thank you!

Emille Bryant. Mentorship comes in many forms, and no one has been committed to mentoring me in life and creativity the way my big brother Emille Bryant has. Emille, your servant's heart, mind, leadership, creativity, and life is a lighthouse on a turbulent sea. I am able to be a visionary, a dreamer, and one who can redefine my own possibilities because of you. Your friendship, brotherly love, creative spirit, and disciplined approach to life inspire me. There's literally nothing I can do creatively without channeling you. I love you and appreciate you and thank you for committing to a ritual that makes every tangible expression of my creativity possible. Asé. ZheZhay!

Thank you Mark Jones for being a real champion and amongst the biggest supporters and practitioners of the Five Lenses®. Nothing works until it is put into practice and "proven" and you've been amongst the biggest risk-takers, consultants, marketers, and salesmen behind the proliferation of every method and framework we've built. I also thank you for constantly thinking deeply about the work we do to make sure every client and practitioner alike experience the purity of what was intended. Few people know how much time, energy, and love you put into everything you do for the people (and the things) you love. I further appreciate the years of friendship, camaraderie, and love that you've offered graciously at every turn. In so many ways you taught me how to live and continue to remind me of what's important in life. Also, thank you for teaching me how to pop bottles in Zagreb, Croatia.

Ronice Henneman, I also can't thank you enough on this page for all that you have been to me as a colleague, friend, and "ride or die" in this world. The "RH Factor" is real between us and I can't imagine continuing in any endeavor without you. Without your steadfast leadership and stewardship along the way, I don't have an organization of any kind to create anything with. I thought about how to describe your importance to me and all of my work and was blessed with the correct term: Professional Soulmate. You're the truest definition of a complementary partner who has given life to everything I've touched.

Thank you Pel for all of the illustrations and for providing the foundation for a series of stories using the Five Lenses that we can build upon. I also appreciate your encouragement to me to finish this small volume and the explicit value you believed the concepts could provide in the worlds of art and fashion. I've spent my professional life trying to find my way back to art and entertainment and you illuminated that pathway for me.

Alex Gould, thank you for your patience and support these last few years as we've attempted to translate every concept, idea, emotion, method, framework, and feeling into a tangible experience. Your strategy, advertising, and marketing talents are unrivaled and your dedication to creating experiences that tell the story of the products has likewise served to make this project (and many others) possible. I also appreciate the subtle ways you choose to ignite my creativity whether through articles and memes you send on social media or design books you send me as gifts throughout the year.

Apphia Taylor for trusting the process and being the first person "on the ground" to put the Five Lenses to test as a tool for technology roadmapping and management and for helping to lend credibility to the practice when you were one of my senior consultants serving the Defense Logistics Agency. Your contribution to the original scorecard we built to measure a program's overall health was a catalyst to our fully understanding the Five Lenses' legitimacy as a framework. We drafted off of your work for a few years and I yearn for the day I have another team member as dedicated, intelligent, and gifted as you were and are.

Andrea Simms for building an engagement model that cleared a pathway for using the Five Lenses as an evaluation tool for clients. Also for your tireless efforts and mathematical brain in helping to develop the ETM Scorecard for our DoD clients. Also for your years of support and friendship.

To the original team of the infamous "VCFIG" responsible for supporting our clients with the Five Lenses and standing up two offices within the Department of Defense with the framework at their foundation:

Tomika Anderson, Dior Richards, Patience Ibik, Trinity Bergeron, Christopher Evanoff, Nicole Harden, Liliana Cruz, Chrissy Floyd, and Tammy Tracey.

Others I'd like to thank in no particular order who either inspired and supported me and/or implemented and promoted the Five Lenses:

PelNYC, Vicentee Ferguson, Niklous Combs, Mark Brahms, Erin McKenzie Brahms, Mike Ness, Amy Choi, Kristanie Castillo, Mike Farley, Martina Johnson, Mark Drever, Brionna'Paris Crutchfield, Jasmine Major, LaQuinte Campbell, Erika Santos, Stacy Bostjanick, Sharon Flowers, Leslie Lewis, Tim Addison, David Retland, Dr. Kelly Page Jibrell, Brendan Epps, Jason Harris, Christian Johnson, Emille Bryant, Winsome Walls, Philip Deboe, Ajay Endlaw, Mike Ness, Roy Apseloff, Donald Adcock, Princess Gunter, Frederick Deese, Seung Lee, Wayne Young, Alexander White, and likely others I simply can't remember in this moment.